SINNER'S PRAYER BOOK

WGD

CALLWYN BOOKS USA

© 2014 Wm. Godding Deckelman
CALLWYN BOOKS USA

*Afore you cast the stone, it read,
adjust the mirror.
Don't hit your head.*

Think of your head, that orb among a billion others, small compared to the globe you live and walk on, large only in comparison to the head of a bug. And you think you're brilliant? Smart even? Wise among men?
Be humble. You ARE humble.
Be thankful. This is your best prayer for being included here among life. And, if things aren't going right, ask help. Ask it with the voice of gratitude.

When everything you do goes wrong, when you are beyond your wits, have crashed from the lofty place where once you dwelled, do what the Lord did: look for ways to help others. Forget yourself. You will find yourself again this way.

Such violence in the world! Such greed, deception. Even money now seems a trick we thought we could count on. What have I done to improve things? And why do I look to the government to make things perfect? Was Caesar a saint?

Holy people are happy ones. That's why sinners are often found among them. And why pious ones who think they're perfect often are dissatisfied hypocrites. Acknowledging weakness is the road to strength.

Beggar
In the quandary
To get, to give, to save
I paid them the honor
To take what they gave

No stop lights for hearses
No strike at the grave
Worker or boss
Slides grease on the ways

Deference on earth
Respect below
Concerns not this crowd
They can't wait to go

To all manner of sorts
To lunch or to sports
Expecting sorrow?
Less tears than warts

Watch them be happy
No time for quartz
High hold your glass
Here's tears, you morts!

Ever likely in life
The heart be light
The music turn loud
The party go tight

Sinners, sinners
Are not we all?
Saints save us at last
The last time we fall

LATINOS
We come to save your land, they said. Hard work we bring, not strikes for pay. We love our families the old fashioned way.

If anyone asks for volunteers, our hands are ready to the task. We love the nation as a mother, and protect her with our lives.

THAT'S HISTORY
Marvelous sights
Ocean views of the sky
In the south Pacific
Astounding the eye
If not for gravity
We might be pulled into it
Then coming out of St. Michael's
Into the Bay
A grand regatta of sails
Varied in moving color
But all has slipped

Slipped?
Slipped through the fingers
And even the fingers will slip
That's history
The fact of people living in time
Yours is galloping
On a modern motionless saddle
Grab, if you can, the reins

If ever I discover a strange new world, may it be a new world of light.

Time itself a wonder:
Slowness becomes so fast
Can no man split two things asunder
And make the fleeting last?

Stars moving brightly
Time is only that
Stops when all is still
The perfect does not change

ETERNAL SURPRISE
Love of neighbor, tolerance, trying to understand difference ... without offense/ it occurred one day from the blue/ that eternity might startle the life out of us/ with sudden knowledge/ that our brother/ our neighbor/ the foreigner/ our enemy/ all/ are only aspects of one person/ and the giving of love/ all along/ had been giving (or withholding it)/ from ourselves

WATCHING GEESE

An early morn
Before the frost
Clouds one color
South to north
Perfect sky
For geese to cross
And here I am
My boat & oars
I started toward
St. Michael's town
Fresh high waters around
Looked again
Up to the sky
And thought: no gear
Had I brought I
Then headed home
There on land
To wonder
How such wobbly birds
At trouble even to stand
Ever learned to fly

When to munch overcomes
Carnality to hug
Days grow caricatures
Of featured mugs
And people ever mindful
What they were
Are stunned to see
That dogs don't really care

15 MINUTE MONEY
Casually count the dollars in
More than need
Is that a sin?
All around I see the same
Every day all play the game
At the end who cares to think?
The suffering suffer
Was I to blink?
Enough I must have
Thought I
To live 15 minutes more
Then die
(Even at a cost so high
In lives of others suffering)

Loud! And from the Dark
Can you stand the sounds
Of war?
Or does clamor no more frighten
As you don't fight any more

And words, the only enemy you see
At home, with the family
Brave talk may end
In dripping blood
You, at home, won't see the flood
Nor, at home, slosh the mud
In a cocoon
Your mind dark & snug

WISE
In darkening days, speech ranks high
Words are meant to modify
What action might the other try
And, so far, nothing happens
The enemy, like an octopus
Spread over the globe it lies
Cautions the harpooner's cast
Lest octopus turn occupi

REVELATION
Comes the day
When ownership will be no more than paper,
Riches easily detachable from the person
Kings will awake to their death
Posers found and slaughtered
Then the inarticulate will of the people
Will be championed
And for however short a period,
Peace will reign
And prosperity for all the human race
Till greed once again rises
And until the Lord tires of it
And again strikes it down

Justice is the law proclaimed (and kept hidden)
It stirs men's souls and pleases God
But the wicked walk upon its golden path
(as spiders choose nets)
Rather than crawl the earth itself

THE GREAT THING ABOUT ANYBODY
If you've ever wondered, you might notice there
isn't anybody just like you.
It's the way with people. Each is different — in
one way, in lots of ways.
You're one of a kind. In a manner of speaking,
an historic person. This is because you are actually
alive in a world that is unlike you. It might mean you
see things differently — pretty, clean, strong, fast,
colorful and someone else might only notice the color.
You may hear a story differently: see bravery and courage.
Someone else may just be scared.

You might be friendly to those who seem to have no
friends, do things before being told, be careful —
even when tired.
You might say hello and not wait for the other. You might
act friendly instead of not interested.
You may tell the truth instead of covering up with
a story.
You could be on the way to be president, senator or
general.
But if you don't get there, you can be sure of one
thing — people will see and respect you for what
you are. For the way you act.
You're different. The only *you* in the world. Be
justly proud of the effort it takes. It is not easy
to be wonderful.
Did anybody say popular? Beautiful or handsome?
Did anyone say rich? Smart? Athletic?
The word is wonderful. Because a wonderful
person is not so easy to find.
You will be loved, more truly, than if rich.

Time stops
when we acknowledge
the least among us.
A mark is made in Heaven
for, this day, we have seen
God.

Time
In a world—a universe --
with stars far -- light years away
Time becomes open, vast....
A thing like a day, no treasure to last

Hold then not to ungraspable hours
Be like the breeze visiting flowers
In and around, gently caressing
Admiring, alert, alive in motion
Passing land, covering the ocean
grateful each second, no second the same

Time
Scenes in our life, no fear of ending
gossamer dancers in a dream
Faces once moving, abundance of seasons
Gone from paths that look strangely new

Hope's all the living can grasp
seeing loved ones once more again
at a time and place – call it heaven
where possible is kin to the true

THIS WORLD
The high military lord had spent the day doing every sort of charitable and religious duty. But on the twilight, he found that he had led his men to none other than the Lisbon Red Light district. Eyes moved wide with questions.

"The day was long," he said in earnest, "but now the eve cometh ... bring on the night!" The door opened into a large room of sensual delight, filled with scantily-clad women, each with her own expression of anticipated joy. The wine flowed as was its reason for being.

The general spoke again: "There is heaven, in which we gladly and fully participated. But there is also this. Here we relax, find our solace, live the other side of the coin. God created both, you know. It is up to each man (and woman) to find a choice suitable — to mix, if be best, Night and Day (Heaven and Hell). Both are here. We choose and choose again. Perhaps we never get finished choosing.

"Both created ... for our enjoyment, enrichment, pleasure and suffering. This is the only world we have. In it, we are given a thousand choices.

"The saint is home in bed; we are here. Tomorrow? Isn't it too early to think of that?"

And the dawn brought no trouble. Not immediately.

LUCK
Beware, even if most worries turn out blank, never take a chance. On the other hand, luck is our unconscious brilliance. Fantasy upstaging the quotidian. The Irish act like they expect it.

MOVEMENT
Every minute something happens
Time itself covers the scene
The old get older — like their machines
The new discover what's already been

REAL TIME
You mix into *helping others*
Seen by these as they might cast
Your image makes a magic turn
You've found yourself at last

HELP DOG
Straight away dog!
I know it's strange
All you need know:
You're a dog
Into the crowd
Level-stepping head
Fearless, a matter of pride!
At this old age
I'd swap in a minute
For your eyes
And a coat
 of that hide
Your mission is meet
On confident feet
... sure not
Along for the ride
Life at its best is
Deep in your chest
Advancing
(Self beside)
Loyalty no question
Each breath you take
Beams away
Full in your eye
We humans note
Our devotion remote
We move with diminishing pride
But you, proud dog
Know the meaning of life
You're alert
And have nothing to hide

SOUL
Visible arena of facts
Glittering, but boring and old
Compared to that uncertain pool
The dark ocean, the soul
Bits escaping the mouth
The few of what's always untold

More than a face, more than form
The person inside may be hidden as night
Like a balloon inflated to impossible height
You look at the seen, but don't see it right

Prejudice proves what we already know
What's easy to recall
Ain't necessarily so

OFF STAGE
Whose hand will comb our hair last?
Commit the whole to the past
Halting a whimper
Forbidding a cry
Leaving us out of next day
They'll try
Perhaps a wind chime
Maybe a hound
Bring fleeting thought of the ground
Care we the spot we lay?
Now among angels
Escaped the clay

BEING AROUND
It's flat, you know, the earth
Flatness is a valid concept:
Ask a mountain

THE MAN
Zest for the seas meeting his lust
Travels sweep the mind of dust
Weary ennui threatens the thrill
Need now what venture failed to fill

True peace, the sound of working bees
Wind light, fluffing the trees
Dreaming *now* rather than past
Smoking a pipe in hopes it lasts
No one scolding, voices low
This creature, man -- humble, you know

SCRIPTURE SUMMARY
Children of God, near his knee
But history recurs such tragedy
No truth of his they ever seem hold
Always that plaything, always gold

ALL SEEING
Look, living creatures
The wonders at your side
And remember, you watch
With the very eyes of God

Questions of children
Pure as honey
Hidden by the "wise"
Under the money

EXCUSE
It matters not our genes
What the environment was or is ...
What matters is whether we
Quietly triumph in this life ...
Or lose the dog-fight
Letting the spider crawl upon us
To feast

STRANGE HEALTH RECORD
Floor unsteady
As a ship at sea
Furnishings floating (already in?)
My walk straight amidst it all
But the couch looks mighty good

Nothing is wrong, I swear it
I'm right as right can be
A hearty breakfast nearer to lunch
The wise prescription at sea
(On 2-21-11, my health diminished)

Alice Cross
We met her at the fair
Among fair faces twinkling
Her water colors there
Ones that took our heart
Ten we bought, most hanging still
And every time we look, we say
There's sweet Alice –
Here, yes, today

REAL
And all the things men say are real
Passing fancies into gloom
And all the real we do not see
Faith, the truth of unseen life
Go on
Do not stop
Outlasting all within our lives
The lie men fear is true
You take nothing with you?
You do

CALL
In disbelieving yet believe
And believing, fail
Clear borne truth
Darkness takes
In mystery, the mind forsakes
And doubts an end
That does not come
The goal of virtue ...
The lux of now ...
Mysterious life
No single road at all
Lowering a friend to final fall
Answer I
What call?

WAITING
Waiting is a happy time
It makes life thoughtful
Longer

PUBLIC ADDRESS
All I know in facing crowds
the hordes, the hungry, jealous, proud
the jingling fun on shopping streets,
the stingy, the newly sad:
Put on a mien of love of self
that makes you love others too
It will not save the world
but incorporates a view
that takes a little pressure off
and certainly helps a few
and in the uproaring process
leaves a distinctive trail
called you

AT THE TIME
Challenges come at inconvenient times. It's easy not to recognize the challenge as anything more than a condition – to be lived with. In dismissal lies the seed of tragedy. A challenge is best faced before it morphs to the impossible.

CONQUEST
Will they keep your land
Twisted free by verse
Till someone finds
A scriptured counter curse?
And the land, as life itself, reverts

So good it is to be with you, Greta mused, as she arranged herself again in the chair. Reality ... how can people be fooled by it? Tell me again about reality.
Reality is like a bald rock, ugly, lying in a desert place too hot for snakes to visit, a place where the sun dries out the flesh in a few hours leaving nothing but skin and bones.

And art, what again is art?
Art is the refuge of people ... people who detest reality and dwell with other people who know the magic of existence permitted those who love life, those who drink the divine wine of imagination, who cultivate the possible as opposed to historical fact.

And didn't you tell me that facts are like ants on an apple? That's why I have chosen to live apart. I can't stand the ants.

But who are you? that makes me comfortable with all this? willing to go over my movies, as though the only life there is?

I am the Baron. You remember, the hotel thief, the one who stole your pearls and gave them back ... when I fell in love with you and saved you from destroying yourself in despair.
Oh, yes, the thief. I know now. I told you you could keep the pearls; I didn't want them.
I know. But I didn't want them either.
Then why did you take them?
You remember, I had to support myself; I was a thief.
But all you stole was my heart.

Yes, we were to be so happy. Then, General Director Preysing had to ruin it all by killing me. Art is so sad, she said. Paused. Then flicked on the Grand Hotel again.

THE WORLD LOOKS ON – EYES OF THE FROG
War, artillery barrages, smart splinter bombs, demolished homes, forced migration of ethnic minorities ... but, should you go so far as open a holding center for refugees, you'll be checked meticulously for number of toilets, showers, good bedding, privacy, adequate exercise, nutritious meals and freedom of information. Non-compliance may mean court action! Please watch yourself.

FULL MOON
Horsing around with enemies
Of a careless little friend
Powers rise at our expense
Russia, China, India, South America
Ascend
In our *dream,* we repeat
Cheap slogans of support
On the *ground* we make targets
Of our men

EVERLAST
Death always the feared
Pushed away to oblivion, a void apart
But can anything from the universe part?

Matter renews, no energy lost
Relax in the skin
Don't think cost
Dead though you be
Dark to view
Rising to life
By a new name
Is you?

OCCURRENCE
Enter budding spring to die
On laden green branches lie
Hear Gabriel's notes blowing shrill?
Does the Harp Angel pluck strings still?
I wait in silence

FACES OF THE OLD
All the ways of knowing
seeing others not know
All the ways of envying youth
youth's spa for the mind
All the ways to resent
people traveling slow
and in circles
All the ways of easing gracefully
into another time

Anything that slips or slides
Anything that drips or drops
Anything cold, anything hot
Anything dry, anything not
When I'm tired and hardly thinking
Anything ... anything gets my goat
If I'm not ready to cope

That's why it's always best
When you're tired – to rest
Because when you're rested
Things that slip, will watch their sliding
Things that drip will watch their dropping
Things cold and things hot
Things dry, things not
And things that blow away ...
No problem being tested
If you're a master rested

STUDENT SUBSTITUTE
This class today is yours to teach
Miss Clancy's off out of reach
(Still her young ones need be fed)
Check her book to guide your head
Remember once you were here
Wiser now with recall near
What you learned – to them – make clear

MAGIC
When you meet someone you just don't like
An inside thing – in you or the other
You can leave it at that, let it harden to stone
Or look for a good point -- one thing alone
Chances are – it's happened before
This foe the friend you were looking for

TIME
Time between another's death
And our own
However long
Only breath of a song

MISTAKING THE HOUR
The prisoner was given an hour of freedom
He dreamed up a scheme to feather his nest
Ignoring family, ignoring friends
The time expired, putting wealth to an end
Many who laughed at the prisoner's folly
Follow his footsteps toward similar woe
The span of a lifetime – not hundreds, not thousands
... hardly here till we go

Agent in Asheboro

Less than coincidence, is when things just happen. You see, occasionally my walk is short, to a burger place outside the gates for coffee. It's always a small one and nothing else.

This lady I noticed, every morning was there, reading her paper, talking to friends ... sipping and biting at times. She was like the Guardian Angel of the place even if she had gray hair and glasses.

It was not right away that we became friends. We both waited for the other to smile or speak. Finally, at the same time, we both did both. We're that much happier ever since.

It so happens the lady, let's call her Diane, is about to move to North Carolina to be near a daughter whose husband's name is Joe. They have no children, so there's lots of time to look after the mother person.

Joe's mother is gone, so he calls Diane Mom. Which does nothing but make the threesome closer.

What's conversation like before dawn in a burger place with few customers? Guess we never thought about it – just talked. Anyway, after Diane returned to the neighborhood from being down to Asheboro picking out a place, for some reason, we started talking about Amazon.

Everybody knows Amazon sells everything under the sun. It was news to me that Amazon sold tooth paste. Yes, Diane told me her daughter introduced her to it there in Asheboro. The best she's ever had. It does things to the mouth she's never experienced. She acted like, if she had nothing to do at the moment, she might dart to the bathroom and use some.

I didn't tell her, but was thinking Jeff Bezos somehow had to hear this. There's nothing billionaires like more than a simple stories with advertising flair. I made a mental note.

Now when I told this lady – Diane – that I had a book coming out, she responded with equal surprise to the discovery of Amazon tooth paste. "Oh, can I get one?" Of course. They told me this morning proofs have been shipped! Certainly you will have one. Great, she said; I'll spread the word to my daughter and Joe, and all around Asheboro. I'll be staying where my daughter knows people from church. This thing will catch on! I promise.

I told her – that this being almost November – having Christmas trees on the cover won't exactly hurt. She

smiled: It might be the biggest Christmas Asheboro's ever had.
She was squeezing the enthusiasm out like Amazon tooth paste.

A need
How it happened ... that it came at all
And here I sit in misery
It's new misery
My working life glorious by comparison
And age ...
Age has its finger here
Thicker is the stirred pot:
Family & friends, gone
The air so close you could climb it
And room
There seems not enough to move
Or so much I'm lost
There is no on-going assurance
Happy permanence
Alone, I seek a miracle – that's not to come
I cry
Alone I cry
For some reason then, I see my hand
The human hand – not reproducible by
engineers or scientists
The simple human hand, a miracle with us always
I got mine from God, I remember
Because I needed it

Maybe a friend will come – a needed one

Maybe sorrow has a boundary
Maybe if I begin to anticipate that friend
Be ready, be ready
Be ready to accept another hand from the same place
I have to believe, because I see
the truth of things – impossibility conquered
simply

as natural as my own hand
Keep looking
With dry eyes, look

TIME
Looking for a clock
High in the sky
Eluded my vision
Try after try
It must be up there
I see time pass by
What a masterful system:
A moving sky

ON & OFF
In the fifties I slept
On the deck of the carrier
It was steel & hard
But the night was hot
I had a long way to roll
Before ever falling off
More likely
I'd be stepped on:
I looked like a
 Shadow

HOW WE'VE BECOME
Exit strategy? Takes too long
We want our ventures to end like games
If the darn thing's longer than Notre Dame
Forget it already, leave be the same
Who ever heard of football for weeks?
We need diversion, too hard on the cheeks
In a throw-away world with packaged dinners
All we need is a field of quick winners

SPEED
It's not a good world that frets
So quick it kills before death
Join me in a secret plan
To kill quick before it kills our land

ARRIVING THE GATE
An easy way to a gate you know
Is not the way you were told to go
Walk 'round the world
Help where you might
Enter tired
In greater delight

FACE
I could save this face
And a thousand die
I could risk it
To save as many lives
A mirror shows
The value of skin
How do I rate the inside?

HEARING
Stop the rush, sit a while
Listen to euphoria not always heard
Can't hear a feeling? So wide & quiet
It hums with the muscles & bones inside
Spirit's message now clear to the flesh?
Relax a moment, rest

GIVE & GET
A statesman saw his value raw
Risked *himself* as the nation saw
Saved a lot of guys from war

Glory's friends are mostly jaw
The sight of damage begets their awe
Stopping short of personal risk
Happy to send in troops

COIN
Give me a coin of courage comingling
With everyday threats we've come to know
Every day is a theater of bravery
But not all the brave show

WAY IT IS

Within a day many things may arouse anger. Dexterity may fail, but more commonly, something will simply follow the laws of nature – too suddenly.

Why be angry with nature or self? Or might it be speed? The blind belief that speed is the division point of competence -- or even intelligence -- compelling us to rush when care is the proper concern.

Always start a procedure with this question: Do I want to break a record doing this? Or stay calm and not break anything?

FESTINA LENTE
The ancients knew –
The birds, the geese:
Hurry goes frantic
Destroys the peace
To gain the results you seek
Be slow to do
Even slower to speak

Sleep not too much
Before the grave
Give God back
Some time he gave
Live lively
Small joys save
"Thanks" is good use
The heart he made

SUMMER
How heavy the air
The mind, the heart
Takes energy to breathe
And more to start
The dog and me lie
Planks of the porch
Watching the sky
Avoiding the torch

*MOVING IN THE DARK
WITH HAWKING
What did God know?
When did he know it?
Before creation:
Of the universe
(with man in it) ...
With this early universe
Does God play dice?
We still don't know
What's going on
Standing we stare
Amid infinite whys
At the beginning – belief?
Or do alibis bite?
My doubts might be wrong
God might be right*

*WATER FOUNTAIN TALK
Mirror, mirror on the wall
Fairest mirror of them all
Show no truth, no harm let go
Be kind on the eyes, I need to know*

THE BIG ISLAND
There, I might have died --
The property I loved
Overlooked Kona, the fishing village
Idyllic scene of dreams
Down the mountain comes
A coffee tree aroma
I want to buy this!
But the office said it was sold
An unseen person -- so bold
Made the same decision as I

I might've grown faster old
With that story everyday told
So I carry it in my investment mind
As a loss I left behind

BIRDS
Startled just before dawn
Singing in response to the view
Not yet seen but coming
Every day seeing it new

The perfect age
You've been waiting for
Here & now relax
Sit yourself upon a log
See the world same as a frog
Rise and know the difference be
The same almost but differently
Then <u>log out</u> for security
Frogs record what'er they see
And post it to the readwood tree

Knowing more is worth the years
Worth the tears
Worth the cheers
But aren't we getting ahead
Of ourselves
With the years?

PERCEPTION
See the skeletal
Inside the face?
Don't you grasp
He's walking bones?
Tucked embalmed
Beneath the flesh
Preserved for some day's stones

TALKIE
I was stopped walking backwards
Into the show
A copper caught the scene in time
The flick not started but a minute ago
In the meantime
I found a dime

HOLDING
Some never did believe
in resurrection
Doing the expected
The easy
The faux heroic
They love the moment
Prize what's almost past
They cannot hold
They stumble into disaster
Dig graves
Beating the air with excuses
Their mirror frames the ghost
of what was almost
But not

NON-SOLDIERS
Why do you insist on wearing a uniform?
In the cover of civilian clothes....

MUSIC/PAINTING
It must take your insides out
Float your soul weightless

AGE

You know there is no perfection in life. To criticize becomes a bit silly. But I will do it, here.

By age, I am old. What I resent is a fatalism the old assume. They step into shoes, old shoes, wear faces, old faces, dress old, talk old, walk old – if they walk at all. They do a lot of sitting and waiting. Waiting to become young again? Waiting for care? Compassion? Be the eternal child, moving in wonderment of a new and ever-changing scene. Ask child questions, admit child ignorance, talk excitement. Do, do, do your explorations. Feel, touch, approach, smile, laugh. See the funny clowns all around. (And in the mirror.) *Count* each moment of health anywhere felt. Give. Give from what you already received. Be grateful for all days given. Act it, say it, let people see it!

You came with a child's pure heart. Walk into the distance the same.

DARK
Tons the weight
Sight a blur
The day long
The hour told
Go from toil's unfinished
work
down in slumber's
blanket fold
Let earth go 'round
on its own
bird & man
flew & flown
Go back to night's
trustful black
awaiting
birth again

NEVER WAIT
Nineteen minutes to wait in line
Like being trapped or even sick
The watched pot might never boil
The waiting hand never sees toil
Days are long
But years seem shorter?
Don't wait for rain
When you want water

LEISURE WORLD
Dove & goose will cross your eye
Step lightly here
Lest one fly

Gardens grace
What lawns allow
In your face
What heaven plowed
Charm of quiet
Glen and rise
Home here heaven
Nature's prize

INSTANT INSIGHT
Steal the fleeting (half life gone)
A piercing blink upon the brain
Count it then or count it never
To flash that blink again

WILL
Leaving whatever
Is left for gleaners
Nothing is nothing
As light slips dim
Were I leave only a bird
Singing mornings
To awake the dark
My soul might look a trifle lyric
Or would they see the sound
as lark?

Am I here? Or just think
I'm here and therefore act like
I'm here. How did I get here?
I grew up 75 years ago.

INTERIOR
If the speaker saw thoughts
As the talk went on
The pompous & proud
Would deflate & be gone

LIT
Seeing dark
Shiver like
There might be light
In far off black
To see the earth
Again as real
Or is it only eyes that light?
Day is born
Of night's long fit
Dream of movement
Desire alive
Buzzing bees
Within the hive
And there!
Flashing far to east
Arms of light
Stretch width to reach
Grab back earth
As it own
Its sorrow glad
Its flight flown
Joy on earth
That all is one
Birds leaping
Their hearts sing
All songs left unsung
Hop within a home of straw
To see again
The left unsaw
Thank a God
This gift given
Given too its echo praise
Light returned
To awe our gaze

JUDGMENT DAY
In froth-headed fervor
At the carnival scene
She was bumped
By a clergyman
Triggering her mean
She scowled at the man
Departing all mirth
Deprived the poor priest
His one feel of earth

INSIDE THE BOX
There are two kinds of German
Rocco was saying
The matter-of-fact
Who take humor negating
And the joyous German
Eyes floating in pools
Of happy-talk
From a stage for fools

I favor the latter
(Life, the Lord's joke)
I hope when passing
I can evoke
From the crowd joining in
One healthy yelp
Now I depart you …
Again, with your help

THE LEVEL
The earth is flat
When you arrive ...
But when you die
Gets rounded out
So you can't step off
How hard you try
Sell your parachute
Flat was a lie

THINKING, our highest mode of motion
Hardest off the mark of status quo
Emblem of an energy-high morning
Honesty meeting nature's need to know

THE MIND
Carry on in a fashion suited
Down from that horse unbooted
And henceforth memories only
are to mount
a steed unseen except by you

EARLY
Ahead I saw his wheelchair
In the dark
And passing, told my suffering
Rather stark:
I pace, to be in step, one ahead.
"It's death," said he, he sat there calm
No dread
"Walk on," he said, "even if you're tired
Stopping is something severe
I've never tried"
I turn, I said,
I hear whistling in the wind
And looking…
See no soul of any kind
"Death," he said,
"Does not sneak up behind
You'll hear the rippling wind
First in your eye
Look ahead
To see what always chased you
THERE! (a pause)
That's why I sit wheeled
Ready to roll
Crashing to a roar I passed my goal
O, fake, those stands
Now you see me walk – (these pushing hands!)
And when light or whistling sounds Alert
I'll drive my wheels
At earth's outstretching dirt
Fear not, man
You see me only in dark
My name is Death
I'll come again in day:
A fluttering lark, no harm in any way"

REGALS
King of candy
Caught in caution
Regal ranks restrain
His glee
Times away in country corners
Lend sweet maidens' loyalty

Tired of hunt afield with dogs
Yet outside he would be
Walked alone in wooded fields
Paused, and talked he with a tree

Then one day a neighbor
Caught him
Tickled at this simple sight
The King responded gentle humor
Saying that tree he liked
Quiet, listening, never bored
Unlike some neighbors
He abhorred

ECONOMY
Drift, people in flow --
Talking and doing, you know
Upward momentum a dream
Letting day follow night as they go

The world works its way like a bag
With two cats not friends inside
Suffering the dark in motion
And move, if the other decides

May my prayers loft high as my stocks
Heaven holds grips on my final box

Looking's one of the likely limits
To seeing all the world has in it
Gazing's good as geezers go
Smiling love lets others know

GENERAL AGNES makes the deals
Sends her army to quiet fuss
Keeps the peace so men can prosper
While hot heads bite the dust

Talk's the weapon men can use
To keep God's anger down
Lower swords lest some be cut
Food, the medicine for roaring guts
Agnes, General, smoothes the ruts

SMALL WORLD
Little reason days as these
To fly a flag above half mast
The world's unreasonable, hateful, low
But what of the neighbor I just passed
Without me nodding to say hello?

METHOD
Ugly world
Of inelegant people
How return
To beauty again?
Look to the future
With a heart of love
Glory in provisions
For the young
Blind to distraction
Focus the near
Bury the money
Escape fear

Is it Arthur, or author?
And if the latter, then it's true I suffer from authorwritis. A common malady among those attempting something, not immediately successful. We are taught the immediate: hitting a homerun, tackling a sure touchdown runner, making a hole in one. The Arthur (author) is not even on the field. Not dressed right, too secluded. There it is: I knew it. Thinking is the whole problem. I should be on the field where the story is -- listening.

I've seen the sticky blood of blown off faces
In my nose, the crisp air of fast-burned flesh
Doctors pulling steel splinters from a child's eye
... now tell me the war was an idea of men with high IQ, from good schools.
That the war is right? Opposition the stuff of fools?
There are times when popes – beforehand – know best.

ALERT
Sirens pierce the ears of elders
Flash the calling to stand account
Over and done, no time for thinking
Does a pebble pause before it sinks?

INDIVIDUALISM
I was in the wind
Of the wind
Blown by the wind
Did I know what I was doing?
Did I know what the next day brought?
Decisions, I thought, were made by me
But my variety wore a uniform

THE ECONOMY failed
But they gave us what we wanted
Was it really feeding greed?

MONEY should have no voice
Speech is a freedom of *people*
Otherwise, voting is unequal

CONTROL
MONEY is the Gold Standard
FEAR is the currency
CHEAP is the trick
That makes us WEAK

ADEPT
I've seen Moose, Geese, Elephants, Deer
The size of their brains not exactly clear
I've seen & sized the heads of men
And results make me favor animals again

Lie down, watch the Shannon flow
Spring comes a sweetness
Let it know you know

USED TO IT
To think of death is think of others dying
For truth be told, we've never died before
Obits there, everyday in the paper
Except one day, we don't see them anymore

High nightmare:
Young feet depart for war
Friends twist, and are no more
A no-name shot!
People caught in the rot
Flash ... a miss
"all we have is *this*"
Rubble end of bliss

Faith
Government takes the task of char-i-tee
The Church entreats it for her coin
Religion becomes largely person-all
Was God just Caesar all along?

Be G'isle
O, come with the song
You like so to say ...
"I can sell them much cheaper
Than I sell them today."

And rhyme so sprightly
I laugh straight away ...
"O the turf ain't food
But gives food away."

Sing me a song
Sad now and gray ...
"Johnny, we hardly
Knew you'r away."

"Fought the British
And for 'em too ...
Lost me left hand
And right leg blew."

Ireland the beautiful
Ireland the true
Your spirit's bedevilin'
Eyes look a man through

quiet lodger
single grave
Care of none but grass

But day once was
I strode above
And feared not would I last

The President *Live* at Fulbright's Funeral
Heads high and camera-ready
The lady too nods well
When came that tone of Amazing Grace
The two heads sing like hell

Later the prayers & holy readings
Looks are more nonplused
Treading the world of ideals
Hurts, as hurt it must

"More by him than any mentor
Did I high office tease"
"O, lift the lid," Fulbright moaned
"That my friend lie more at ease"

*Let's get dirty before Jesus comes
Ere we look down even on Him
With hands & shoes all too clean
What did the teachings mean?*

*Holding ALL as a single thing
Does exquisite thanksgiving bring*

Definitions:
REAL ESTATE
How does a Christian hold real estate?
Like in the dark ... a mouse: Have I got it?
Always in the end, I don't.

POLITICIAN
Representation is the job
And some groups demand more than others
Democracy is not a *lay back & watch* pastime

NEW
What I know I know is old
But all is new:
The world's the same

IRISHMAN
Dancing
Floating the music
Man soul & spirit

TRUTH
If it's true, we do not devise truth but live within it
Why do we fear find it? Even look?
Why would we make counter investments?

WORK
If you let things go, they're always finished
Once you start, it never ends

Pause
Bearing life, having it – now
See the eyes of deer or cow
Where is it from? Can we even wonder?
Breathing & breath: put not asunder

MARK OF DISTINCTION
I dispute with my fellows
Whether to depart
The matter of euphoria
Health of the heart

Contention's a maze
Ever re-winding
Contenders go blind
They also try hiding

The right or wrong --
Any major question
Has room for a yes
And acute indigestion

LEISURE WORLD
Sometimes I walk around in this park
Where animals live, especially in dark
The speed I make is slow for the road
From their point of view, I'm in turtle mode

Peace
A measure of slowness
Resounding in pulse
Speed lights the sparklers
And not much else

Soundful

Three miles tired, the mind is not
The sky has clouds and no birds sing
A deer pauses and moves away
The moon is light pale gray

Who won this peace where crickets dance
To tunes they make for silent ears?
Was it always here?
To shatter fears?

Sleep, on till sunrise then
When things here now must be seen
And things as real are hiding safe
From those who only dream

Why's the world adverse to peace?
A thousand venues no one tries
Where dead men walk unannounced
They've not even died

PUB
A friend I wrote on the old sod & safe
Come over, he said, there's a pub near the gate
Join the fun, with freedom to vent
Use your taxes here on nothing but rent

The only cop joins right in the fun
His ticket book's fat: hasn't used No. 1
Don't mention his wife and start a war
That's not what pubs in Ireland are for

Hours pass, the Blarney thick
The clock's hidden, no minutes tick
Happy times leave no room for blue
If you're ever in heaven, remember you knew

Passing
*Death has no waiting
No lines
Nor challenge at all
Before you might care?
You're already there*

Problems with Problems
*There are two ways to deal with reality:
There's the real way...
Well, shall we stick, for now, with that?*

If it's war, it can't be modernity. Or is there no modernity?
No hero comes out of the closet during maneuvers. Who's
brave and who's not is never known ... until.
You can't tell by how people <u>look</u>, or even how <u>you</u> look in
the mirror, that you are not a hero.

Changing your mind – bad? The first thing the
successful leader must have is the courage and wisdom to
revise thinking when new information comes. Are schools
and colleges to reinforce the habits of childhood?

Art is not about talent. Art captures, in the everyday, the
eternal. Our lives can paint, by way of love, and grace of
fearlessness, such masterpieces as we set out to choose.

Failing
It is comforting to recall that earth will never be heaven
and that facing unbelievable clashes, in which we fail, are
also instances of enlightenment and growth. We have
renewed our fire and commitment. We walk on, in a world
a bit more real – and *we* are more real. Salvation, after all,
is becoming true, in the midst of fake imagery and bogus
sign posts.
Like St. Paul, we arise. "And when I am weak ... then am I
strong."

I see the meadow, imagining the Meadow Queen
But in the fog, where is she?
And in the garden ... the angel moving about?
The mist is too great. The distance receding

I forgave that guy
Who shot me in the heart
I shoulda kept cool
The most living of arts

Twice I thought to hit back strong
And remembered history's junk yard song
Shall I suffer the insufferable minute?
And look to a future with me still in it?

WORK
Jobs, the concern
Too many un-working
It's no longer the nation
We lived in before
In spite of our wars
And curbs on inflation
When we go seek a paycheck
We find a closed door
Something is wrong
A man mused in a factory
He turned to his companion
On the factory floor
But stopped – mouth open
Quick as begun
The companion, a robot
Said nothing but "hum"
This is outrageous
He realized at once
Work's being done
By an out-and-out dunce
Which raises the question
Of work at all:
In an automatic world
Where's toil?
Man, obsolete?
In a world just for rich?
Maybe it's time to sew our own stitch
The solution is creed
High finance we don't need
Nor money, if we trade 'mongst ourselves
We can beat this game of greed
Working like a nation of elves
God didn't make the economy
We can change it without enslaving ourselves
Let's use the brain He gave
And re-build the Home of the Brave

Thanksgiving Day
May the Day find redemption
in our deepest selves,
new determination to soldier on
and ease our expectations
of a world not always our friend.

Speed *is the wind carrying good things, past*
Slow, *history's usual speed*

LOOK
I know what you look like – your body
And I'm learning what you look like –
Beyond
When I like what's beyond even more
I love you without looking at all

Trying
A poet can't say what desperately must
Mind is a place of special trust
Things inhabit that hate to leave
Not say, not even breathe

See?
I jumped one day from under a rock
Fit in the world – nary a mock
Folks seemed to see all in light
But light doesn't see the dark it might
And seeing's not all that makes sight right
Even the dark brings things insight

Escape
Brittle bones, buildings fall
Soft stuff melts into cracks
Can spirit be crushed if it stays in place?
Or must it try more supple shacks

Jotting
Can you possibly imagine behind smiling eyes
That granddad, uncle, granny, aunt
Had a life not far from your own
With harrowing tales, as would redden your bones
But they sit listening to you
If only you knew their adventures, my dear
They didn't write them down

(Present)
The trouble with the present
We think it's now
Present is the cloud
We couldn't grab hold
Through the fingers gone
Disappears at night
Entices again in the morn

Under the skies
Were the clouds
And under the clouds
The wood
And under the wood
The earthen ones
Who sought to be understood

St. Joan at the Inquiry:
Blackbirds, a row facing the child
Waxing their victuals of scholastic pride
A sparrow no more to frighten or kill
What wit might she show?
How bright flash her will?
This session of pick-bones
Waits only the grill

Warriors
The feel of strength, legs and arms
Volume in lungs and voice
Confidence built by the sight of it all....

> But no bird lights on a shoulder singing:
> Frailty
> Pride without substance
> Tiredness untimely
> Error irretrievable

Little consequence, a simple slashed artery
till it's your own artery slashed

Down. Out, before time was full
Lying flat, mouth-open awe
in a valley, looking up with the mountains
under a sky blowing sweet common flowers
in silence watch the doings of men...
Silence, silence, till the Lord comes
Smile faintly, not jolly
Speak meekly of folly
A warrior's end is no fun

Blessed the eyes
In other eyes looking
Whose thoughts are
Further away than now....

The dream of tomorrow's
Tomorrow...forever
Forever a love
Our eyes show well

A breeze lights the cheek
Whisks the hair a little dumber
But who would care? It's summer!
Life inhales fortune forever
Believing
there's small chance of change

When body weakens
Toward the dusk
Spirit loosens
After its run
As night pulls sleep
Over the flesh
Life on earth
Is one

Comfort comes
Upon the soul
Which has beforehand
Spoken prayer

The gift of wealth
Is commonplace
Peace of mind
Is rare

Am I alive?
Or think so?
Pieces of time
What are they?
When I was sitting *there*
Drinking coffee ...
Did time elapse without me knowing?
That was 20 years ago!

Impossible the date it is!
A miracle –
On top the past

What'll we ever have
in movement like this?
Actors in a play
Beginning to end (five dollars)
And how much they pay
For one more day

COGITATION
A fish in the water jumped in the boat
What 'e wanted, he said, was a chance to float
'e had read about ease in a travel book
Was still on 'es mind when the chance 'e took

The thought was still in 'es mind, it was
The thought was still in 'es mind

It's same with the bloke
With 'es hand in the air
Catching the waitress – unaware
Wanted another drink, 'e did
The thought was still in 'es mind

The thought was still in 'es mind, it was
The thought was still in 'es mind

No more comely maid 'er entered the bank
And the banker's eyes upon 'er sank
He gave 'er a rate she couldn't refuse
Cost 'er more, the more she was used
O, the thought was still in 'es mind

When the thought is still in the mind
When the thought is still in the mind
What might we do when our thinking locks
Is something out there beyond

THE SHORE
Moving, deep power, moving
I'm a pawn in a motion-master sea
Beach people lounge the warm sands watching
Me, ready to drown

GLARE
The News generates forgetting
Slogans hold unmeasured views
Privacy slips with the coffee
Nothing seems worthy of new

REAL TIME
Mixing in with needy people
Feeling the woe they cast
Unseen your image changes
Finding yourself at last

WAY WE'VE BECOME
Exit strategy? Takes too long
We want ventures to end like a game
Anything longer than Notre Dame ...
Forget it already. Leave it the same
Who ever heard of football for weeks?
We need diversion -- too hard on the cheeks
In a throw-away world with packaged dinners
Don't field an army if they're not quick winners

CHANGING MORE THAN APPEARANCE
Perhaps it's time to go unicameral
Stop humping it with a House
Democracy lasts only so long
Ask a holy one
Ask a mouse

This place has a second shift?
Can these be represented too?
I ask this as a fellow member
Of a distinct malodorous zoo

Till then, sew on the patches
Of every interest served
Mobil, for Mobil Oil
Chase, for a Wall Street curved

Let them appear on TV screens
Blazoned as daredevil drivers
Laughing stock of the nation they serve
Truth is the last survivor

COULD BE WORSE
On the ground, the fog was thick white. You couldn't see the earth. And higher, more fog still, but smoky – you saw darkened tree branches, bare and eerie because that was *all* you could see.
As I walked along – and how I walked I don't know; there was little evidence of a path – I wished for a cat, a dog maybe, something to give me a measure of companionship. There was none.
How on earth I got here, did not seem so important as moving on ... in hopes of getting out.

There was plenty light but nothing to see, except more bright fog, more snow, a silky carpet. Just a glimpse of dirt (I say dirt because there couldn't be grass in such a place) would add a measure of confidence. Then a pool of water appeared. There was a small dog – a comely little puppy, drinking. I said to myself, how queerly she takes water: not from the top, but about six inches underneath. Stepping nearer, I saw what was happening. There was a bowl on the bottom and from this, the dog was lapping. How very odd! Lifting her head periodically into the air and thinking to herself, no doubt, this was perfectly natural.

It was strange, but not quite so as what was next: a bird (black of course) hanging by its wings over limbs and kicking its feet while issuing a most bizarre squealish song. I asked the lady there about it and she smiled and said nothing. She kept smiling, indicating a message of pleasure and assent that I was there, but not a word said.

It was a mile more, it seems, before the little man raised his hand. I took it to mean what is universal: stop. "Can I go out?" I asked. "Have you come across the little dog?" "Yes," I said. "Have you seen the hanging bird?" "Yes," I said. "Did the little old lady speak to you?" "No," I answered.

"Then you may go," he almost shouted with a displeased face. I paused only for a moment before stepping back into the world of hate, jealousy, fear, violence and deception. What a wonderful world it is!

Count in Days
You, of course, know how old you are. But how many days is that? How many times did the sun rise, day stretch out, night come ... and you learned little?
Don't count years. Fifty-five years, for instance, is 20,075 days. Look at each hour. Hold it in your hands. Eternity has already started. Savor it.

Being in command's the hot seat
People look up for your nod
Keeping on top is exhausting
Need a break & my fishing rod

CASINO
Slapped his coin on double zero
Watched, the wheel was spun
Eyes big as the wheel he saw
A singing blur of fun
Paid before & covered cost
Hope was breathing wild
Reds & blacks chased around
The wheel slowed from loud
Everyone here still had a chance
The motion hushed the crowd
"Double zero's inching"
"Double zero near top"
Double zero! Valiant knight ...
Dog, you dog of click-clicking song!
You clicked one click too long!

O time
How you split eternity into this and that
And shock us with the change

There's no way that *seeing*
jumps the gap to done
But work *began*
when seeing had its fun

To converse
Is the other side of contemplation
And shows the character
Of private thought

In a sack, the placenta of the living world
We grow, test and become wise
Move our arms in abandon
Then stare through photographs
Into the next age of action
Those who do not know they are captured ...
Except a few
Finding a door through art and science
To shout what they found
For everyone coming after

Cloud cloud drifting by
Time enough for every care
But I remember things undone
Lazy minutes one by one
People whose time is gone
Clouds without a mouth or horn
To warn
Our moments going, gone

"Once were here"
They all all said
The moment the moment
They saw themselves dead

BIRTH OF IRISH FREEDOM
When the guns went quiet
They wobbled out the battered building
Sleepless
Into the larger cage of British sovereignty

This handful
Unsupported by countrymen
Mocked even
Saw daylight scold their dream

How foolish
How pregnant the scene
Bitter was God's work in '16

LOVE

Love is an ancient Irish way, of picking flowers while gathering hay, of cracking turf so it shows a smile, of walking above the road for a while.

Ned
Arisin, oh, in the black of marning
Putting on his smelly coat
Ned's a fool, a working wonder
... is all the Lard musta wrote

He cleans of the cow
Feathers a foul
Walks to the store
Smokes up a cloud
Mends the shed ...
(if he wouldn't wear his clothes to bed!)

Sitting by the fire his lady
Rubbin her head in her hands
For the ways of Ned are free
A life his dog understands

How time makes prophets of the wise
Stealing thunder from the freely-mouthed

Being is our concern
Using every high ideal
The way the coffee's lifted
How we treat the server

Fix your glasses, cross your legs
Sit back in assurance of a civilized world
About which you can do nothing
About which you feel it's the best
And on which you exert no pressure

OFFENSE
... be like Joyce, carry hurt
like a blanket to the grave?
... Fly away bird!
I want fresh air
My toes in the sand
A man
Unhurt by hurt's hand

REVIVAL of the FITTEST
Renouncing by total attitude any thought that possessions, entertainment or a world of diversion can satisfy the primal urges of humans ... for friendship, relevance, being part of something timeless & strong, actuating ourselves by the spirit in us and responding to the spirit in others ...

... when all is said and done, it is the motive power within us we will be judged by (and will judge ourselves by). Did we use it? Did we even recognize it as the most important part of us?

Rise up! Let your you-ness shine – always and everywhere. Others will forget your car, house and maybe the exact way you look. But they won't forget you – if you show them exactly who you are!

Raise not a fist to the sky
but a waving hand
And say, Yes, to those who spot us,
it is I

DON'T LET REVERENCE STOP YOU
Think about it: At the Last Supper
The Apostles were with a friend
Someone they were drawn to
They ate a meal
They *talked* to Christ
They did not pray to him

If reverence puts Christ
In the category of the unreal
Be frank
Be street-familiar
But, if you must pray,
Remember – don't embarrass a friend
With words you wouldn't say

How time does make an ancient of us all
And fool the young who have not felt its grip

A Christmas Story

O power of a simple scene, a vocal sound ....

When I was a boy, the rent collector one day had the discourtesy to say that his mother was so clean he didn't dare wear shoes in the house. It was an obvious reaction to the untidiness he was presently witnessing.

"That's nothing," my 12-year-old brother Martin said, we don't even wear shoes outside"!

"Hush," mother scolded as she pushed Martin back away from the hearth, his eyes growing larger as he sensed he had said something wrong.

The rent collector sat back in his chair musing, and he gradually was overcome by the warmth. "In recognition of the season," he said to my mother, "and with Christmas so near ...." He went on to say he would not raise the rent by half, as was right, but only by a quarter.

"Raise it at all and you'll have Sean to deal with," said mother. "He's away hunting with friends, but when he comes back, I'll lay that on him – on his boisterous, drinking self. And I'll tell him, and I don't mind telling him, where, if he's got a shot left, he can get one most handsome weasel."

Her heavy brogue caused the message to sink slowly into the rent collector's head. And when he gained sense of it, decided to act as if he hadn't. He merely answered "Good day, ma'm," and sauntered off to a place where his horse was having a shoe fixed.

On the way, he met what had to be my father's (Sean's) loud-laughing hunting party, whose happy spirits were quite irresistible to this lonely, workaday businessman. In the worse way he wanted to join them, but knew he'd never be accepted. So he walked on. But not without this thought burning a new trail in his cold mind. From this day on, the rent collector decided he would celebrate life like Sean and his friends. Yes, he would even drink, if that helped. And yes, he would become one of the "people" if that were necessary.

When the rent collector reached home much later that day, he sat down and penned a note to Sean: "Nollaig shona duit" he said, which means Happy Christmas. "I'm fortunate to have such tenants as yourselves. Be assured rent on your house will not be going up this year at all."

The rent collector loosened his tie. Oblivious of his wife, he began examining a bottle of Bushmills his grandfather had given him when he turned eighteen.

Fisherman's Throw
Pick the target
Raise for the cast
Strange resistance
The hook caught my ass
Now I got three flys
One I could spare
But it's better 'n
Catching the damn thing
In your hair

Sometimes I think I should have stayed in Washington and become a lawyer like my father, or gone to Wyoming to college (instead of Houston). The cobbles I've traveled, the fields I've crossed, the lakes, the streams ... how the weather's beat down upon me! The people I've perceived in all these movings ... this is what's been responded to and why I wrote.

All the other paths, would have meant other writings ... of which, of course, I know nothing.

It's sad sometimes not to be like God.

THE CIVIL WAR
Then moved the troops
From out the field
Between the dead
As scarecrows
Between corn
As woeful as forlorn
Days are bright, bold & long
Nights are short with summer warm
Something in our eyes has changed
The war has made us old

RICHMOND ROAD
In these woods once was wars
Woe and footsteps rustled leaves
Birds were frightened from the trees
Fallen men like fallen logs
And the night song still was frogs

Clamper feet
Dust rise smoke
Night's ahead
Many have last awoke

Dead lie a wreck
happened quick
Names – no matter
Tom, Jake, Mic
An hour ago
They dreamed of sleep
Sleep has them now
Cold in its keep

Guns worn
Rusty to your grip
You had no mind of mercy
But then
What mind you saw in other men?

Adrenalin and prejudice
Poor substitutes for discretion
Disaster in the night seeks fatherhood
And wisdom ...?
Is it ever born a bastard?

Slow down, passion
Your answers come too soon:
What you render mornings
Must be swept by noon

SOLDIER'S PAUSE
Human cause
That I fall for ...
In a forsaken field –
(Not even a good look at the enemy)
My friends are scared, solitary
They hardly notice me gone
Stubborn helpless pain ...
Here in the country
Where children will come
And not see or hear anything
Am I a fool? I ask the knowing dead
The living go on groping
For what a 1,000 times might be read

THOUGHTS OF WAR
Walking with my feet
Upon this plain
With fear that makes the weight
Of arms seem light
Glimpses of too-soon coming night
Admiring lives of birds
Dogs, mice
Who do not have
This reasoned mode of vice

SOLDIERS
Many feet march the battle
In earnest, clash & be cut
When a king's embarrassed
And finds himself in a rut
Violence, the only reply with clout
Men not missed when not about
Droplets off the hand that grips the sword
Takes a thousand common men
To make a lord

PALLBEARERS' REVOLT
We refuse anymore to carry the dead
Laid low on *brave words* said
Quiet patriots from anywhere in the land
Consigned by cowards quick to the sand

HAPPY BIRTHDAY, RITA

If travel makes you younger
This can't be too soon
In both hands take a bag
Walk out towards the moon

Give kind regards to Snuggles
Wave to passersby
Don't stop for anything
Till you're up in open sky

Eat with friends & talk
Enjoy as once you did
Get younger by the minute
And keep your troubles hid

PRAYERTYME
Life could be the long dear truth
Were not it yanked like a common tooth
On and on we dream it go
(people die we don't even know)
Life is our life, we mean
Death defied every day we see
Till strength of limb is our limb
Then call we the Lord off the tree

DEPRESSION
Though darkness hide where footsteps go
Ahead I move as in the light
Daytime's strangers do not know
My eyes see only night

VERNACULAR
Believing he's off in clouds somewhere
It seems all right to pray
But when you meet him face to face
You might have something to say

THE GREAT NEED FOR RELAXATION
Nixon was good
His enemies knew
They led him a dance
He made his own stew

DAY
Tangled branches dark & brooding
Chirping birds hear the dawn
Night is moving over mountains
Light sees a forest born

JUSTICE
Intelligence is a fallible knower
Convinced of truth
And often wrong

COMBAT ZONE
In plain day
(like a man shooting a cow)
The advancing soldiers paused
blew up our house & car
while we watched
as would watch workmen
It did the loss no good
to think how news of this
step-by-step process
would be reported
Glamorized as "war"

O war
Our fingers sift your dust
You are common ... too like
Things we already know

BUSH
Thanks to Osama bin Laden
With condolences to the recent dead
I am a man who leads
You, my people, are led

Doubts to this lay of land
Crept bitingly at the edge
I phoned my friend Saddam
for support
(so came his threats alleged)

Reactions are very predictable
When you're top dog head of state
Saddam blew a fit in public
And we met at the world's back gate

(Were it any other world ...
Any other day ...
I'd have a smaller stadium for my play)

But Grant didn't look like a president
Nor a general, others would say
He conquered war – with war
When fame, with a squint, turned his way

Any store clerk or sportsman
If his country issues a call
Can jump in the boots of the best
And rip through the world like it's small

No way to tell, fellow countrymen
Who's hidden there in the crowd
Someone standing next to YOU
Might someday rise like a cloud

Play games with my Texas tongue-tie?
(not exactly a man of words)
But when the pot's all boiled out of water
They'll say what he knew
Was verbs

SONG OF GEORGE
Of a man I sing
Leader, no king
By swagger & temper
More like emperor
For his force was felt
'round the world

Peace his cry
And by war he'd get it
He'd choose enemies
To later regret it
A fearless man
The most guarded on earth
His courageous threats
Brought the enemy's mirth
Took a nation near solvent
Into outrageous debt
At the polls, by golly
A two term bet

DON'T FORGET
A day is blue
Is blah
Says end
Only until you spot a friend
Delight is the vision
You find in eyes
The very first thing
A smart dog tries

GOLD
When money is divorced from gold
And based instead on belief
A nation becomes religious
But not to God's relief

GOSSIP
How else does one learn errors and achievements
of those who will never make the news? Ears cock, voices
descend to whisper.... A tiny morsel of irregular behavior
has power to bring the world to silence.

RAMBLING THROUGH
Life is a chance, a thousand chances
To say to the world
I was here

Find a way to love all
Let loose spontaneously and clear

Glory in the presence of everyone
Trust in hearts of the near
Earth, garden of wonders
Seasons help minds forsake fear

Arise, ye spirits
Into things that
May be dreamed

My heart is like Kilroy
Waiting everywhere
Expecting you

Ongoing work's no adequate cover
The Irish respond to life like a lover

SAVE
How step amid potholes
not playing coward or fool
living a life half-Christian
within a soul gone cool

At every turn – money
safe in its blanket of dark
a blinder-hood against evil?
but evil sees its mark

Our Christ, lamb and leader
yields to suffer with grace
Trust in his words, however
is at odds with the human race

Save? Salvation? Savior?
From what, we ask in pride
Look 'round about you
Tragedy doesn't hide

PERPLEXED
If we value the dead
And can't risk peace …
Our values are
In line with our fears at least

TRIPPING IN GEORGIA

Jeff: You will not believe this, Rocco. While I was in Georgia last week, a tire went flat and forced me into one of those rural country gas stations where, the first thing you know walking in, is that you're different. Every smug face begins its oblique but studious observation.

Rocco: I think I know the situation.

Jeff: The first guy I deal with has this laid back rush of an expression and asks, in a low-motivated monotone: Hep ya? I tells/tell him about the tire. And he says Bubba will help me on that, pointing to the other guy sitting near a potbelly stove with his feet up. When I sees/see Bubba I blurt out something to the effect that I'm on a trip and would like to move right on, quick as I could.

Rocco: So what happens?

Jeff: Bubba tells me the other guy would have to write up a work order ... 'cause he don't do nothing without a work order. So I ask what's the other guy's name and he tells me Bubba. Bubba? I thought you were Bubba. I am Bubba. You mean there's two Bubbas? There's two Bubbas but only one Buddha ... if you can keep that straight.

Rocco: What kept you from walking right out?

Jeff: My flat tire.

Rocco: Were there no other places?

Jeff: Not like this one: I was so interested now in the story here that to leave in the middle would kill any anecdotal reminiscences. So I play on.

Bubba, I say to the first: Bubba over there needs a work order. Bubba's supposed to tell me that – not you. You work here??? Sorry. Hey Bubba, you have to tell him yourself.

Rocco: Sounds like you got yourself flat in middle of a redneck hornet's nest.

Jeff: So Bubba No. 2 yells it across his own self. And I stand there watching the face of Bubba 1. There was no reaction. He just wrote up the thing as if he heard the boss say to.

Rocco: Who WAS boss?

Jeff: I was thinking they were partners but the Bubba with his feet up was probably boss, so I start to call him Boss, and he answers I ain't no boss. Bubba's the boss. I was terribly relieved to get that straight and began thinking about my tire again. Then came the revelation of the day: Tires are sent out. We don't do them here. But you can pay here. Have a seat. Unless of course you want to do the work yourself. You can use our tools at no extra charge.

Rocco: Now I know you left.

Jeff: Not so quick, Rocco. I remembered I had not asked what the price might be. And the first Bubba, after telling me the other place would have to determine that, suddenly, in a fit of entrepreneurship, tells me I could buy a new tire quicker -- for only a hundred and fifty complete. And you would put it on? No, Bubba would do that. Seeing I was in the middle of a profit-motivated triangle, I says: Would you consider a hundred even, if I promise to advertise your place up and down the road every trip I make?

Rocco: This I got to hear.

Jeff: Bubba says, Man, we got so much business, advertising's the last thing we need. So, Rocco, I bought my most expensive tire ever.

Funny thing was, I was almost home when that tire blew, right in front of a gas station. The guy told me I was lucky not to be killed: the tire must have been carrying 70 pounds pressure to blow like it did.

Rocco: I'm sure those Georgia fellas were honest, my friend. For $150, they knew they owed you something more than just a tire. And air was the first thing they thought of.

IRISH BLESSINGS

May your bark show smiling teeth
Your tumble through life
Find you ever on your feet
The better the new & strange to meet
And finally, the Lord greet

Rocks, the rugged wrath of Eire
Pinch of spirits by the fire
Night among a singing choir
Countrymen! Happy they are!

More soothing than low Irish skies
Is the room I find in your own dark eyes
The feeling we share – not even a word
Cozy and candid, not taken for granted
Bless our little ole home

May the intervening trivia of your life
Be as beautiful to the eye
As the carefree moves of a puppy

FINAL
Funeral words
Very odd
Love the living
The dead are God's

If at funerals
There be said
What had to wait
Until he's dead …
Ask forgiveness

SAINT PAUL
Not so much a soul
Stuck in a body
But a spirit
Flown out

***P**ride has no substantial structure*
It has no roof --
vacant lonely ruin in the atmosphere

Art and writing pass through
Like food we covet not

VACANT EYES
The earth has erupted: see the buildings
Pushed up from expanding pressure
Alike, with a variety of difference

Windows galore, vacant panes
If only someone looked out
For clouds or rain
If only buildings looked like people again

WHAT?
God's more good than we are bad
Forgiveness means life can go on

Hate eats five meals a day

Freedom equals forgiveness

Chaos is a fear relationship

Duty is being your best self

Love is not letting the bite of pain
register on the face of another

La Mancha

La Mancha is not for real men
Battle's no thing of a dream
A sword in the hands of a warrior
is awesome, better shined and kept clean

In fields where fight might be joined
The clank, the bang so close
scarce an arm lifts its metal
than ten arms swing metal at once

Eyes without fear look quickness
(fear flies away in the charge)
Motion rules once you're in combat
(God hates stomachs too large)

But tiredness resides under glory
And when glory herself becomes tired
The ache of a thousand tart hits
Sound a pulse to the ear of the heart

Heroes carried without walking
Back to the honor of kings
Scarce said are prayers and priest words
Than sleep steals away glory on wings

Only fools fight the thought-wars of La Mancha
whose enemies are surprised to be foes
Where war is declared in an instant
when someone steps on our toes

Battle's no thing of a dream
Swords better shined and kept clean

How Not to Live a Thing like Life

There is something to be said about an examined life ... before it's almost over.

Richness – ready and waiting – is staggering. And compared to the rat race, it's remarkable so few stop, look around, and say: by golly, this shit has to stop!

Don't be offended; our society is full of it. It doesn't have to be. Merely a pause, a quiet retreat into the solitary, may be enough to lift the soft barrier separating cultural chaos from an ordered dignity *becoming* humankind, perhaps intended for our species.

Compared to what?
Changing how things are done makes waves whether it's job routine or some procedure at home. That's why routines are commonplace.

A guide book only reaffirms the pain, and most are pains themselves. Examples already existing are better and more easily accepted. That's why, in changing the order of life – hold your breath – the monastic life of the middle ages might be looked at. See, if from the refreshment of this plan, you might acquire unanticipated order and tranquility worth millions.

If only a foothold is gained, it may be a foothold you enjoy *daily,* an oasis in time, an ownership beyond mere property.

the rule
Simplicity is not a word ... it's a concept. Pervading the ordered life, it orients self to the rest of existence and God. It unifies a person to everything else, as it relegates the person to dependency *on* and responsibility *to* others – a humble position, which experiences pride more in belonging to it all, than in the self having a personal and *exclusive* relationship with the creator.

Things are important but things can wait … for their time to be accomplished … created (in cooperation with the creator). When you work your best, there is no deadline, no overtime. You do not fret, you are not anxious. Go merely to the next order of the day: prayer, study, recreation, service to others. There is plenty time. All can be done within it, moving evenly at diligent speed. When the hour comes to sleep, nothing else is proper. Relax, forget labors, your cares – leave all to God & sleep with clear, light mind. Into the heavens till morning … angels watch you!

Life's too valuable to use up like a commodity, as though opportunities to *begin* were *unlimited,* as if ungrateful for what can easily be beautiful, exciting and full of quietly observable wonderment.

You are the *kind abbot* of your life. Take every advantage to enhance it on the road through time. (Earth has no meaning in personal chaos.)

Valentines is every day
A heart ready, words to say
Locking tight what just might drift
Thorns from little rose buds sift

Every day comes just once a year.
It is not always evident what makes it special.

BLOWING CHANGE
Move ahead, wake the dead
Sound the bugle, beat the drum
Facing the foe
Is a battle won

America,
Captive in a night of many fears
Slipping through fingers (digits) go our hope
Relaxing under slogans, we have moped
"Wise" men grab the cash and steering ropes

Is our worklife encrusted in the past?
Do we have to wait a new dance till we're asked?
Must we incite the Moslem world
To ways not perfect here?
Expecting magic's blink?
Don't we know modern power's at the top?
Democracy, a word and likely flop?
Pull a bone from the dog who knows it's his?
Or is peace the price of leaving as it is?
Foreign friends history shows can turn
And enemies once, become the best, we learn
Discourse, rigid in its prose?
America, blow the cobwebs from your nose!

Dead Poets Laugh Last
The last page in history
Spare me time to write
Dogs yelping loud
Words all too trite

I can't give up unfinished
But nothing works the same
Outrage roams the streets
Wisdom has gone lame

Skies tell the story
No one wants to hear
It's all over, Joe
The end we fear is near

If ever in a dream
Sweat melts on the brow
You know the absent feeling
Of power to save us now

Not visible is heaven
All looks too close to hell
No time to prepare
Nothing has value to sell

Caught with emblems of worth
Burdens unworthy of weight
Walk away to somewhere?
Take me to your gate

What is prayer but thought… pious or not, for the good of the world, if not self. This world needs it as a start toward better acceptance, kinder treatment, happier people.
What if everyone in the world was poor and hungry? What if just the opposite? And what would that cost? During a life barely 100 years, even the well off would be happier.
Courageous means doing the brave thing differently.

SEE SPAN
Roust the spirit
The flesh desire
Rake the soft
Soul on flies
Left to earth
Memory dries
Gone a'breeze
A day went by

Laugh the little laugh
(Truth displayed)
Mind the spirit
Unannounced in other ways

INDEX
Of Titles and First Lines

(Present), 71
15 Minute Money, 8
A breeze lights cheek, 74
A Christmas Story, 89
A Thing Like Life, 110
Adept, 57
Adrenalin & prejudice, 93
Age, 42
Agent in Asheboro, 28
Alert, 56
Alice Cross, 19
All Seeing, 17
Am I alive? 75
Am I here? 45
America, 112
Anything that slips, 26
Arise, ye spirits, 102
Arriving the Gate, 33
Art and writing, 108
Art not about talent, 66
Arthur or Author? 54
At The Time, 21
Be G'isle, 59
Beggar, 4
Being Around, 16
Being In Command, 80
Being is our concern, 85
Big Island, 38
Birds, 38
Blessed the eyes, 73
Blowing Change, 112
Bush, 98
Call, 20

Casino, 81
Change Appearance, 78
Changing your mind, 66
Civil War, 92
Clamper feet, 92
Cloud cloud drifting, 83
Cogitation, 76
Coin, 34
Combat Zone, 98
Conquest, 22
Control, 57
Could Be Worse, 78
Count in Days, 80
Dark, 43
Day, 97
Dead lie a wreck, 93
Dead Poets, 113
Definitions, 61
Depression, 97
Don't Forget, 100
Early, 49
Economy failed, 56
Economy, 51
Escape, 70
Eternal Surprise, 6
Everlast, 25
Every day comes, 111
Excuse, 18
Face, 33
Faces of the Old, 26
Failing, 66
Faith, 58
Festina Lente, 36
Final, 107
Fisherman's Throw, 91
Fix your glasses, cross, 86
Fulbright's Funeral, 60

Full Moon, 24
General Agnes, 53
Give & Get, 34
Glare, 77
Gold, 101
Gossip, 101
Great Thing About Anybody, 10
Greta, 22
Guns worn and rusty, 93
Happy Birthday, 96
Hearing, 34
Help Dog, 14
High Nightmare, 58
Holding all ..., 61
Holding, 41
How We've Become, 32
I forgave that guy, 67
I see the meadow..., 67
I thought to hit back, 67
I've seen sticky blood, 55
If at funerals, 107
If I ever discover, 6
If it's war..., 66
Impossible the date, 75
In a sack, 82
Individualism, 56
Inside the Box, 47
Instant Insight, 44
Interior, 45
Irish Blessings, 106
Irish Freedom, Birth, 83
Jotting, 71
Judgment Day, 47
Justice, 98
Knowing more is, 39
La Mancha, 109
Laugh the laugh, 114

Latinos, 5
Leisure World, 44
Leisure World, 63
Let's get dirty before, 61
Level, 48
Lit, 46
Look, 69
Looking's one of, 51
Loud! from the Dark, 8
Love, 84
Luck, 13
Magic, 27
Man, 17
Mark of Distinction, 62
May my prayers, 51
Method, 54
Mind, 48
Mistaking the Hour, 28
Money, 57
More than a face, 15
Movement, 13
Moving with Hawking, 37
Music/Painting, 41
My heart like Kilroy, 102
Ned, 85
Need, 30
Never Wait, 43
Nixon, need for relaxation, 97
Non-Soldiers, 41
O time, 81
O war, 98
Occurrence, 25
Off Stage, 16
Offense, 86
On & Off, 32
Ongoing work, 102
Pallbearers' Revolt, 95

Passing, 65
Pause, 62
Peace, 63
Perception, 40
Perfect age, 39
Perplexed, 103
Prayertyme, 96
Prejudice proves, 15
Pride no substance, 107
Problems with Problems, 65
Prophets of the wise, 85
Pub, 65
Public Address, 21
Questions of children, 18
Quiet lodger, 60
Raise not a fist, 87
Rambling Through, 101
Real Time, 13
Real Time, 77
Real, 19
Regals, 50
Revelation, 9
Reverence Stop You, 88
Revival of the Fittest, 87
Richmond Road, 92
Saint Paul, 107
Save, 103
Scripture Summary, 17
SEE SPAN, 114
See? 70
Shore, 76
Sleep not too much, 36
Slow down, passion, 93
Small World, 53
Soldier's Pause, 94
Soldiers, 95
Sometimes I think..., 91

Song of George, 100
Soul, 15
Soundful, 64
Speed, 33
Speed, 69
St. Joan, 72
Stars moving, 6
Strange Health, 18
Student Substitute, 27
Summer, 36
Talkie, 40
Thanksgiving Day, 69
That's History, 5
There's no way seeing, 81
Thinking, 48
This World, 12
Thoughts of War, 94
Time itself a wonder, 6
Time makes an ancient, 88
Time, 11
Time, 27
Time, 31
To converse, 82
Tripping in Georgia, 104
Truth, 62
Trying, 70
Under the skies, 71
Used to It, 58
Vacant Eyes, 108
Valentines is, 111
Vernacular, 97
Waiting, 20
Warriors, 72
Watch Shannon flow, 57
Watching Geese, 7
Water Fountain Talk, 37
Way It Is, 35

Way We've Become, 77
What is prayer, 114
What? (definitions) 108
When body weakens, 74
When to munch overcomes, 7
Will, 45
Wise, 9
Work, 62
Work, 68
World Looks On, 24

www.ingramcontent.com/pod-product-compliance
Lightning Source LLC
Chambersburg PA
CBHW061331040426
42444CB00011B/2862